THE SMELL OF POO CLOSED PARLIAMENT!

The fact or fiction behind **LONDON**

Adam Sutherland

WAYLAND

First published in paperback in 2016 by Wayland
Copyright © Wayland 2016

Wayland is an imprint of Hachette Children's Group
Part of Hodder & Stoughton
Carmelite House
50 Victoria Embankment
London EC4Y 0DZ

Editor: Debbie Foy
Design: Rocket Design (East Anglia) Ltd
Illustration: Alan Irvine

A catalogue record for this book is available from the British Library.
ISBN: 978 1 5263 0066 9
eBook ISBN: 978 0 7502 8723 4
Dewey Number: 942.1-dc23

Printed and bound by CPI Group (UK) Ltd, Croydon, CR0 4YY
10 9 8 7 6 5 4 3 2 1

MIX
Paper from
responsible sources
FSC® C104740
www.fsc.org

An Hachette UK company
www.hachette.co.uk
www.hachettechildrens.co.uk

All illustrations by Shutterstock, except 4, 15, 20-21, 39, 41 and 77.

THERE ARE LOADS OF WHOPPING PORKIES TOLD ABOUT THE UK'S CAPITAL CITY...

read on!

Read this bit first...!

Here's something that might surprise you: some of the things you've read about London aren't true! They are often myths that have been passed down from generation to generation — that are simply wrong.

Sweeney Todd
The Demon Barber of Fleet Street

But here's something that might surprise you even more: some of the things you read about London *are* true! And it might be that some of the weirdest and tallest tales that are actually facts.

So how can you tell which is which? It's a simple as picking up a copy of **TRUTH OR BUSTED** *The Smell of Poo Closed Parliament* and flicking through these ever-so-entertaining pages. Let this book be your myth buster, your metal detector on the beach of truth, your truth-seeking missile in the battle against falsehood, your... well, you get the picture.

TRUTH OR BUSTED *The Smell of Poo Closed Parliament* covers some of the most popular stories about London. Is it true that Sweeney Todd (pictured left) turned his victims into pies? Did the Great Fire of London only kill six people? Is the statue in Piccadilly Circus actually called Eros? Everyone thinks they know the right answer to these questions — now you will for sure!

Apart from the surprising truths, and unexpected falsehoods unearthed in this book, we've also collected together some fascinating Cockney rhyming slang phrases, listed some of the dirtiest and most dangerous jobs that Londoners have ever done, and discovered some inventions that you would never in your life have thought were born in Britain's capital city.

The next time you're face to face with a know-it-all spouting some old London myth, put them straight. No need to thank us — we're just doing our job...

read on!

So you might hear myths like...

> ## only six people died in the Great Fire of London

The whopping blaze that swept through the city from 2–5 September 1666 was so awesomely large that it came with its own permanent capital letters so people would remember it. The Great Fire of London started in a bakery on Pudding Lane and is estimated to have destroyed the homes of 70,000 of the city's 80,000 inhabitants. However, the remains of only six bodies were officially recorded. How on earth could such a massive blaze only have killed six people?

⭐ And the truth is...

Historians draw a distinction between how many people are likely to have died, and how many deaths were actually recorded. The figures differ by several thousand. They think this is because a) deaths of poor people were often not recorded, and b) the fire burned at such extreme temperatures that bodies were completely incinerated.

Verdict: _(exact number not known but)_

'WOULD YOU ADAM AND EVE IT?'

COCKNEY RHYMING SLANG EXPLAINED

Rhyming slang started in the East End of London around 1840. No one's really sure if it began as a harmless rhyming game, or a way of talking in code to fool non-locals. New rhymes started cropping up from the mid-1850s onwards and are still being invented today.

So if you hear:

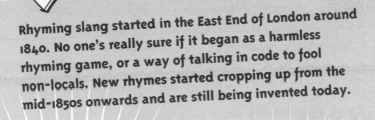

'Old Harold couldn't Adam his mincies!'

Adam = Adam and Eve

Rhymes with believe

Mincies = Mince pies

Rhymes with eyes

So 'Old Harold couldn't believe his eyes!'

'Did you visit the baked's house when you were in London?'

Baked = baked bean

Rhymes with Queen

So 'Did you visit the Queen's house when you were in London?'

> # Every year, nine double-decker buses' worth of fat is removed from London's sewers

Has your mum ever told you should always run hot water down your sink when pouring away cooking oil or fat? These are both liquid at room temperature, but if they cool together they can congeal and block your pipes. Mmm, maybe that's just our mum.

★ And the truth is...

Some old wives' tales are actually real! When substances like cooking oil or fat from a frying pan are poured down the drain — particularly in the huge amounts used by restaurants — they do indeed set solid when they cool, and can cause severe blockages to pipes. This leads to overflows and in some extreme cases even flooding.

Thames Water, who maintain London's Victorian sewer system, have a BIG job on their hands clearing accumulated fat from the capital's sewers, which is collecting quicker than they can remove it. Even with a full time clean-up operation in place, these blockages cause flooding to 7,000 houses per year!

So the clear out happens every few weeks. Just don't expect to see any London buses going down the road filled with fat — lorries are more practical!

Verdict: _____ TRUTH

© MADE IN... LONDON!

'Anyone for erm... sphairistike?'

No.1: Tennis

Or should we say 'sphairistike' (pronounced 'sfee-ris-ti-ki') — the name given to a new game with racquets and balls invented by Major Walter Wingfield in London in 1874.

The Major pinched a few elements from existing games: the net from badminton, the ball from a game called fives, and the scoring system from racquets, and named his new sport after the Greek phrase 'sphairistike techne', meaning 'the skill of playing with a ball'.

Luckily for us, Major Wingfield decided no one would remember it, and changed the name of his invention to 'lawn tennis' instead!

> **Sherlock Holmes author Arthur Conan Doyle lived at 221b Baker St, the same as his crime-fighting hero**

Like 10 Downing Street, 221b Baker Street is one of the most famous addresses in London. The building is now home to the Sherlock Holmes Museum, with its first floor living room preserved exactly as it would have looked in Victorian times when the brainy crime fighter would have been in his prime.

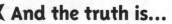

★ And the truth is...

When Conan Doyle wrote his Sherlock Holmes novels, the street numbers on Baker Street only went up to 85, so 221b was a fictional address. The street was eventually extended though, and in 1932 a building society moved into offices from 219–229 Baker Street. For years, they had to employ a full-time member of staff to answer letters addressed to Sherlock Holmes!

Verdict:

'WOULD YOU ADAM AND EVE IT?'

COCKNEY RHYMING SLANG EXPLAINED

'Put the stinger on, I'm thirsty'

Stinger = stinging nettle

Rhymes with kettle

So 'Put the kettle on, I'm thirsty'

'Are you coming for a ball around the park?'

Ball = ball and chalk

Rhymes with walk

So 'Are you coming for a walk around the park?'

Real lions (not just statues) used to live in Trafalgar Square!

The four lion statues in Trafalgar Square were designed by the painter and sculptor, Sir Edwin Landseer. He actually requested casts of real lions to be delivered to his London studio so he could perfect his designs. But what's all this about lions on the loose? Surely the only chance of central London being overrun with wild animals is if they escaped from the zoo?

Grrrrr...

⭐ And the truth is...

Back in prehistoric times, the whole area that now makes up the capital was home to all sorts of wild and dangerous animals! When the foundations of Trafalgar Square were being built, hundreds of strange fossils were dug up, including the bones of lions, elephants, hyenas, bears, bison and even huge hippo tusks. So lions did indeed roam the land of black cabs and double-decker buses!

Verdict: ———— TRUTH

'WOULD YOU ADAM AND EVE IT?'

COCKNEY RHYMING SLANG EXPLAINED

'You should have seen his boat when I told him!'

Boat = boat race

Rhymes with face

So 'You should have seen his face when I told him!'

'John's always been a good China to me'

China = china plate

Rhymes with mate

So 'John's always been a good mate to me'

THE DEMON BARBER OF FLEET STREET MADE HIS VICTIMS INTO PIES!

First things first: was Sweeney Todd, the demon barber of Fleet Street, *actually a real person*? Boffins are still debating this, but we're convinced by the evidence of crime historian Peter Haining, author of *Sweeney Todd: The Real Story of the Demon Barber of Fleet Street*. Haining pieced together news articles from the time and reckons that not only was Sweeney Todd real, he polished off at least 160 victims over 17 years!

Haining claims that Todd was born in the slums of Stepney in 1756, and was orphaned at 12 years old. He was then taken in by a 'cutler' (someone who makes and sharpens razors), which is where he learned his deadly trade. After a spell in prison for theft, Todd set up his own barber's shop next to St Dunstan's Church in Fleet Street. No one knows why he began killing his customers instead of shaving them, although it was probably something as simple as robbery. When he was eventually captured, the police found his house full of the valuables he had stolen from his victims.

⭐ And the truth is...

Allegedly, Todd's barber's chair tipped up and dropped his victims head first into the cellar underneath his shop. There he would slit their throats, and cut up the bodies — taking the heart, liver and kidneys to his girlfriend Margery Lovett's bakery in nearby Bell Yard.

The murderous pair didn't bake enough of their victims, though — it was the smell of rotting corpses that eventually attracted the attention of the police. The pair were arrested in 1801 and Todd was hanged in January 1802 in the grounds of Newgate Prison. And please, no jokes about close shaves!

Verdict: (enough evidence to make us believe it's) **TRUTH**

THE SMELLIEST JOBS IN LONDON!

One thing's for sure — London in the old days was the poop capital of the world. It seems that people were either collecting it, shovelling it, or wading through it. Here are some of the jobs that would have required a large clothes peg over your nose...

1 Human 'portaloo'

Before the days of public lavatories these folk walked the streets of London carrying a large black cape in one hand and a bucket in the other. Whenever the average Londoner needed the loo while they were out and about, paying a farthing (about a quarter of one pence) would get them a bucket to sit on, and a cape to cover their modesty. After all, it's not like people want to be watched while they're pooing in the street...

2 Pure finder

There's always money to be made out of muck. Or in the pure finder's case, dog poo! The pure finder collected dog poo off the streets of London and sold it to leather goods makers for the equivalent of 10 pence per bucket. The leather makers, or 'tanners', coated the leather in dog muck, and the alkaline in the poo would soften and season the leather before it was turned into anything from a pair of shoes to a book cover. Note: You'll notice we didn't opt for a leather cover on this book!

3 Muckraker

Not to be confused with Bond film *Moonraker*, this person had a rather less exciting job. Before the days of pavements and regular rubbish collection, with animals wandering the streets and citizens throwing their waste out of their windows, it was impossible to walk down a London street without stepping in something nasty. The muckraker came to the rescue, sweeping a path through the waste and manure so that people could cross the road without hearing a horrible squelch.

4 Gong farmer

This exotic-sounding name was given to the men in Tudor London who cleaned out the toilets of posh houses. Even rich people's lavatories were just holes in a plank of wood over a pit, and the gong farmers collected the contents when they were full and carted them outside the city walls to dispose of them. The pong of the gong was so bad that gong farmers were only allowed to work at night, and had to live in a separate part of the city where their whiff wouldn't upset the noses of posh folk. Phew-y!

> Whoopsie, I've dropped me glasses – now where are they...?

You're never more than 10 feet from a rat

Rats are the source of some brilliantly yucky facts. Did you know, for example, that a single pair of rats can produce 2,000 babies every year? That there are more rats than humans on the planet? Or that they pee an extraordinary 80 times per day?

But the question isn't how gross are rats, it's how many are there, and how close are they to you?

⭐ And the truth is...

In Britain there are an estimated 60 million rats. That's one rat for every person. In London, the figure goes up to 1.3 rats per person. With an estimated seven and a half million rats in Greater London, with area of 600 square miles, it means that there are 12,500 rats per square mile. That's a lot of rats, but of course rats tend to live outside or in sewers. So even though statistically speaking, there might be a rat every 2.5 square feet, they tend to hang out together rather than spread out. So you may spot a few rats, but you'll often be more than 10 feet away from one.

Verdict: _____ a little bit true — but mostly

'WOULD YOU ADAM AND EVE IT?'

COCKNEY RHYMING SLANG EXPLAINED

'I've been having terrible trouble with my Hampsteads'

Hampstead = Hampstead Heath

Rhymes with teeth

So 'I've been having terrible trouble with my teeth'

'Put a clean dicky on for school today'

Dicky = dicky dirt

Rhymes with shirt

So 'Put a clean shirt on for school today'

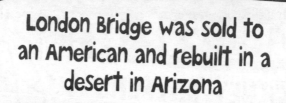

London Bridge was sold to an American and rebuilt in a desert in Arizona

*'London Bridge is falling down,
Falling down, falling down.
London Bridge is falling down,
My fair lady.'*

We've all heard the nursery rhyme, and actually there are times when bridges over the Thames have got a bit crumbly and needed replacing.

Bridges have existed on or near the site of London Bridge since Roman times, with the first stone one built in 1176 and lasting a whopping 655 years! This was knocked down in 1832 to make room for a wider and stronger bridge that was able to cope with the increase in traffic into the City of London.

By the late 1960s, however, the replacement bridge was also ready for the bulldozers until one bright spark said, 'Hang on a minute, we could sell this!'

⭐ And the truth is...

London Bridge was indeed put up for sale, and was bought by American oil millionaire Robert McCulloch for $2.46m (£1.58m). The bridge was taken apart brick by brick, with each piece numbered for easy reassembly like a massive Lego kit. McCulloch rebuilt the bridge over the Bridgewater Channel Canal in Lake Havasu City, Arizona, where it's now the centrepiece of an English theme park — together with a Tudor-themed shopping mall. Apparently, the theme park is the second biggest tourist attraction in Arizona, behind the Grand Canyon!

Verdict:  TRUTH

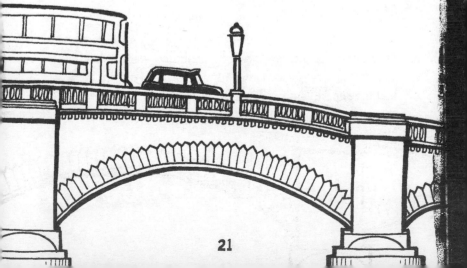

> # The names 'coppers' and 'the old Bill' came from London policemen's original truncheons

So the story goes, in the early days of the Metropolitan Police in the 1830s, constables carried truncheons with a band of copper at one end and the royal initials WR — William Rex — stamped at the other. Hence the two nicknames that have stuck with the police ever since.

★ And the truth is...

Like a lot of great stories, we *want* this to be true, but there's just no evidence to back it up. Historians can't agree on the origins of the word 'copper', although most believe it has been around for a hundred years longer than the truncheons we just mentioned. Some think it comes from the Latin word 'corpore' meaning a group of men, while others believe it's short for the words 'constable on patrol'.

As for 'Old Bill' — the Metropolitan Police list 13 possible sources for the name on their own website, including the fact that the laws the police enforced came from 'bills' in Parliament, and that the department's original car number plates all started BYL, so the squad became known as 'the Bill'.

Verdict: A little bit true — but probably  **BUSTED**

'WOULD YOU ADAM AND EVE IT?'

COCKNEY RHYMING SLANG EXPLAINED

'Are you telling me porkies?'

Porkies = pork pies

Rhymes with lies

So 'Are you telling me lies?'

'I've known him ever since he was a dustbin'

Dustbin = dustbin lid

Rhymes with kid

So 'I've known him ever since he was a kid'

The statue in Piccadilly circus is called Eros

Some things we just take for granted without questioning them — the earth is round, the sun rises in the East, and that angel, firing his arrows across Piccadilly Circus is Eros, the God of love. No need for debate. Or is there?

⭐ And the truth is...

Doh! The statue known as Eros is actually a memorial to the 7th Earl of Shaftesbury, a famed philanthropist (a person who gives money to good causes), and is actually not Eros at all, but an angel representing Christian charity.

Don't worry, you're not the only one fooled. The Victorians were up in arms when they saw a naked cherub plonked in the middle of London. Only over a period of time, did the public's affection grow for the statue. During the Second World War it was evacuated to Surrey to avoid bomb damage, and every New Year's Eve it's boarded up to stop revellers clambering all over it and bending the angel's bow. Ouch.

Verdict: BUSTED

© MADE IN... LONDON!

● No.2: Pavements

Until the mid-eighteenth century, London had no pavements at all. Horse-drawn carriages would rumble through the streets, squeezing through the smallest spaces between buildings and forcing pedestrians to jump for safety or risk getting squashed.

That was until 1761 when a carriage containing the Speaker of the House of Commons, Arthur Onslow, got stuck tight between two buildings on Craig's Court, close to Trafalgar Square. Try as they might, the carriage driver and footmen couldn't free the carriage, and a hole had to be cut in the roof for Onslow to escape.

The angry Speaker stomped back to the House of Commons and immediately voted through a law requiring all householders in London to pay for a row of kerbstones in front of their house. The pavement was born, and carriages haven't got stuck since.

25

> # A glass of London tap water has already passed through nine other people

So the story goes, London tap water is used and reused so often that you might as well go and drink out of a muddy puddle than risk filling a glass from your kitchen tap.

We drink it, we wee it out, it goes down the toilet into the drains, gets purified and ends up back at your tap again. Urgh! Not exactly appetising. But that can't really happen, can it?

★ And the truth is...

All tap water — whether you're in London or Land's End — has been used before. However, before we pass you the sick bag, it's worth pointing out that the actual proportion of water that might have been drunk before is tiny. Of the 150 litres of water each person uses every day, only about two litres is drunk, with the rest being used for showers, baths, washing machines, dishwashers and so on. Is that worse? We're not sure!

Verdict: - **BUSTED** - (but still slightly sick-making)!

© MADE IN... LONDON!

Cor blimey! I'm a fashion model, ain't I?

No.3: Fashion models

The first fashion models weren't six-foot-tall catwalk superstars, but six normal girls from Bermondsey, hired by the fashion designer Lucy Christiana Sutherland aka Lucile, to show her clothes at the world's first fashion show in 1899. They were labelled by the press as 'Lucile's mysterious beauties'.

Lucile sold her designs to the A-listers of the day, including members of the Royal family and stars of the theatre. Lucile's 'mannequins', as they were known, strutted their stuff at invitation-only tea parties, with music performed by a live orchestra. So not only were fashion models invented in London, but fashion shows too!

IS IT A SAUSAGE?
IS IT A GHERKIN?
IS IT A TENT?

London's most oddly shaped landmarks

30 ST MARY AXE

Never heard of it? That's because it's the official
name for the strangely bulbous London skyscraper
nicknamed the Gherkin, which is a large green pickle
that most people take out of their hamburger before
eating it. Designed by famous architect Norman Foster
(the building, not the pickle) it was opened in 2004, and
has even featured in Hollywood film **HARRY POTTER
AND THE HALF-BLOOD PRINCE.** As itself.

THE SHARD

Under construction at the time of going to press, Shard
London Bridge aka the Shard of Glass, will be the
tallest building in Europe at 310 m (1,017 ft) tall when
it's finished. The building will contain 26 floors of
offices, restaurants, a hotel, a spa, apartments and an
observatory at the top! Not bad for a great big pointy
glass thing.

THE 02

Originally built to commemorate the new millennium, and named the Millennium Dome, the 02 was regarded as a big round waste of time and money until it was renamed and rebranded in 2007. Since then, the 02 Arena has become one of London's biggest live venues, with a capacity of 23,000. If you want to see Rihanna, Coldplay or X-Factor Live in a huge tent with yellow poles sticking out of it, this is the place to go.

CITY HALL

City Hall squats on the south bank of the Thames near Tower Bridge, looking like Darth Vader's discarded helmet. It is the headquarters of the Greater London Authority (GLA), meaning it's where the Mayor works when he's not out on his bike. Again designed by Norman Foster (City Hall, not the Mayor's bike), it was opened in July 2002.

The Gherkin (aka 30 St Mary Axe)

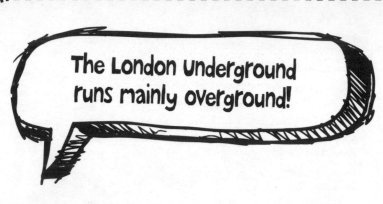

The London Underground runs mainly overground!

It's hard to believe that the London Underground is nearly 150 years old! Today, it is a major business with three million passenger journeys made every day, serving 275 stations and over 400 km (250 miles) of railway.

The Metropolitan line opened in January 1863 and ran nearly 6 km (4 miles) linking the mainline stations of Paddington and Farringdon. To build the line, engineers used the 'cut and cover' method. Streets along the route were dug up, tracks laid in a trench, covered with a brick-lined tunnel and the road surface replaced. The roadworks stopped traffic and hundreds of people were evicted from their homes to make way for the building works.

Underground or overground: the facts

Line	Route Length	Underground	Overground	Stations Served
Bakerloo	23 km	11 km	12 km	25
Central	74 km	23 km	51 km	49
Circle	21 km	18 km	3 km	27
District	64 km	17 km	47 km	60
East London	8 km	4 km	4 km	8
Hammersmith & City	27 km	12 km	15 km	28
Jubilee	38 km	19 km	19 km	27
Metropolitan	67 km	10 km	57 km	34
Northern	58 km	39 km	19 km	51
Piccadilly	71 km	21 km	50 km	52
Victoria	21 km	21 km	0 km	16
Waterloo & City	2 km	2 km	0 km	2

 And the truth is...

As the tube network has expanded to cover over 400 km (250 miles) of track, engineers have only dug underground as a last resort, and have tried to keep tracks above ground whenever possible — it is safer, quicker and cheaper to build and maintain. So today only around 45% of the London Underground runs underground!

Verdict:

Passengers can't sit in the front seat of a black cab

Hackney cabs, to give them their proper name, have been around in one form or another since the days of Oliver Cromwell. Of course, the first cabs were horse-drawn, and historians believe the name Hackney either came from the area of London that produced the best horses, or was an Anglicised version of the French word 'haquenee', which was a small, well-trained horse.

With all this talk of horses, perhaps it's not surprising that the following rumour appeared: you can't sit in the front seat of a black cab, as by law the driver is required to leave the space free for a bale of hay!

★ And the truth is...

Sorry, but this story is horse food. Actually, even when taxis were horse-drawn, the driver was never required to carry a bale of hay in his cab. The front seat of a Hackney cab is kept empty for security reasons. The driver sits upfront and doesn't want to risk being robbed or assaulted by a criminal passenger.

Verdict: **TRUTH** (but for a different reason)

© MADE IN... LONDON!

No.4: the Valentine's card

St Valentine's Day has its origins in ancient Rome, with citizens celebrating the death of an early Christian, not surprisingly called Valentine. Fast forward to 2010, Valentine's Day is big business, with an estimated one billion cards sent!

The first recorded written Valentine's was sent by Charles, the Duke of Orléans, nephew to the French king, in 1415 while a prisoner in the Tower of London. The Duke was captured at the Battle of Agincourt and passed the time in jail writing romantic verses to his wife in France. Around 60 of the Duke's poems can still be seen in the British Museum. Which makes us think his nasty jailers never delivered them to his wife. We hope he took her flowers when he finally got out!

Criminals are still hanged in London for treason

Treason is a fancy way of saying that you are planning to kill your King or Queen, or do something to damage the safety of your country.

A person who commits treason is called a traitor, and traitors have traditionally been treated severely. From the thirteenth century anyone found guilty was taken to one of several sites around London and hung, drawn and quartered — a truly nasty way to die (see following page). There is even a Hung, Drawn and Quartered pub near Tower Bridge, close to one location where traitors met their gory end.

 And the truth is...

The Treason Act of 1814 changed the punishment for treason to death by hanging or beheading. Beheading was abolished in 1973, but hanging remained active until 1998 when the House of Lords voted through a change to the Crime and Disorder Act. At that time the death penalty was abolished for treason and replaced with a sentence of life in prison.

Verdict: **BUSTED**

GRUESOME WAYS OF BEING KILLED

HUNG, DRAWN AND QUARTERED

Prisoners were hanged until they were nearly dead, then had their privates cut off and their stomachs pulled out and burned. After that, they had their heads chopped off, and their bodies cut into four pieces.

Gruesomeness rating: 3 out of 3

BEHEADING

A quick blow with a sharp axe doesn't sound too bad, does it? Unfortunately, axes were often blunt, and an inexperienced executioner might take several blows to separate a pesky head from its body – with the victim still alive!

Gruesomeness rating: 2 out of 3

HANGING

As far back as the twelfth century, criminals were being hanged in London at the Tyburn gallows, close to the site of Marble Arch today. Executions were open to the public, and hundreds of people turned up to watch. Prisoners died of asphyxiation (lack of oxygen), which took a good few minutes of hanging around!

Gruesomeness rating: 1 out of 3

The smell of poo once closed Parliament

Make no mistake, for hundreds of years London was one of the pongiest places on the planet! Horse manure piled up in the streets, people threw their household rubbish out of their windows, and toilets in many homes were little more than a hole in a plank of wood with a bucket underneath.

Then flush toilets were invented! Brilliant, everyone thought, and goodbye to the pong. Wrong! Modern-day sewers collect waste and transport it to treatment plants, but in those days, toilet waste was flushed straight into cesspits (containers built to hold toilet waste). These cesspits couldn't cope with the increased volume of water and started to overflow. Human waste ran into the street drains and from there into the Thames!

⭐ And the truth is...

In the hot summer of 1858 London experienced 'the Great Stink'. The Thames was blocked by overflowing sewage, and the smell from the river was so eye-wateringly bad that MPs in the House of Commons considered relocating upstream to Hampton Court for a few weeks. However, heavy rain hit the capital (what's new?) and although the pong lessened, it prompted Parliament to push through stricter laws on drainage and public sanitation. Hooray for that!

Verdict: A little bit true but mostly **BUSTED**

The children's rhyme 'A ring, a ring o' roses' is about the Black Death

'A ring, a ring o' roses,
A pocket full o'posies,
Atishoo, atishoo we all fall down.'

We've all sung it in the playground, but we bet at the time you had no idea that this children's favourite was associated with the Great Plague that wiped out 20% of London's population from 1665-6?

In the last 50-60 years, historians have pointed out that a rosy rash on the skin ('ring o' roses') could be a symptom of the plague, that a 'posy' or bunch of herbs was often carried as protection, and that sneezing, coughing and, yes, falling down were what you did before you dropped down dead!

And the truth is...

Nice idea, but not true — for several reasons. First of all, this version of the rhyme has only been traced back to 1883, and in fact the original rhyme only dates back to the 1790s — over 100 years after the Great Plague hit London. Also, phrases like 'falling down' are more likely to refer to curtsying — something common in a lot of singing and rhyming games of the period.

Verdict: — **BUSTED** —

Beefeaters got their name from eating beef

The Yeomen Warders (Beefeaters) of Her Majesty's Royal Palace are the Tower of London's own in-house security force. Established as the Royal Bodyguard by Henry VIII, their job was to guard the tower and to make sure no prisoners escaped.

Today 38 Beefeaters are still in post. Since there are no longer any prisoners to watch, they spend their time as tour guides and posing for photographs with the tourists. And presumably still tucking into plates of roast beef to live up to their nickname.

 And the truth is...

Actually how Beefeaters got their nickname is still a mystery, but most historians believe it was dreamed up by jealous locals because part of the Yeomen Warders' pay came in the form of rations — beef, as well as mutton and veal. Fresh meat was an expensive rarity in Henry VIII's day.

Verdict: A little bit busted but mostly  TRUTH

Trafalgar Square was never actually finished

Trafalgar Square has to be one of the best-known tourist attractions in the whole of Britain, not just London. In 1838 a group of influencial businessmen, peers and Members of Parliament commissioned a lasting monument to Lord Nelson's victory at the Battle of Trafalgar 33 years earlier. The centrepiece was the 145-foot high Nelson's column, surrounded by four lions designed by sculptor Sir Edwin Landseer. Surely we would have noticed if it wasn't finished?!

And the truth is...

In each corner of Trafalgar Square there is a plinth, designed to have a statue standing on it. In the northeast corner, there's a statue of George IV himself, in the southeast corner it's Major-General Sir Henry Havelock and in the southwest corner of the square it's General Sir Charles James Napier.

The fourth plinth in the northwest corner was originally intended for a statue of William IV but the money for the statue could not be raised, in part due to the King's unpopularity! This plinth has housed several temporary exhibits, but nothing permanent.

Verdict:

LONDON'S MONUMENTS

Cenotaph, Whitehall 11m (35ft)

Victoria Memorial, Buckingham Palace 25m (82ft)

Albert Memorial, Kensington 54m (176ft)

Nelson's Column, Trafalgar Square 61m (200ft)

The Monument, London Bridge 62m (202ft)

LONDON

THE MOST DANGEROUS JOBS IN LONDON!

You wouldn't believe what some people had to do just to earn a crust in the olden days!

1 Watermen

For 600 years until the 1800s these early taxi drivers rowed passengers up and down the river from Kingston to the City of London. They even had to double as stuntmen, riding dangerous rapids through old London Bridge as the Thames raced through the many small openings. One mistake and they risked destroying their boats and drowning!

2 Limelight men

Victorian Londoners loved the theatre — and the more extravagant the better. Most theatres employed special 'limelight men' to work on special effects. These chemical-juggling daredevils heated manganese dioxide* in a sealed bag to produce oxygen, then mixed it with hydrogen from another bag to produce bright lights. Limelight men could even produce different colours by varying the amounts of oxygen and hydrogen they mixed. Get the mix wrong and you've got a dangerous and explosive mix. Boom!

*A mineral compound used today in batteries

3 Toshers

Have you ever dropped something valuable down the loo or the sink? Well toshers were the people who went hunting through London sewers by candlelight scavenging for the gold and valuables washed up down there. It was easy to get lost in the vast and winding Victorian sewer system, and even if you made it back to the surface you would not only smell rotten but also run the risk of catching typhoid or some other horrible disease.

4 Searchers of the dead

This lovely sounding bunch actually went from house to house looking for plague victims. For every one they spotted, they earned four pence. The victim's house would then be boarded up and the rest of the family quarantined too to try and prevent the disease from spreading. If you spent your time visiting plague-ridden households, chances were you'd catch it yourself, so the job wasn't the most sought-after position!

Plague doctor's special anti-plague outfit...nice!

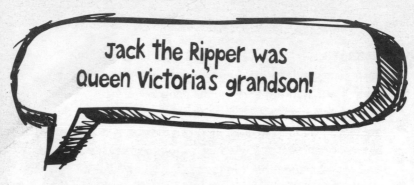

Jack the Ripper was Queen Victoria's grandson!

There are very few criminals who have fascinated the public for more than 100 years, but Jack the Ripper is one of them. For a period of four months from August to November 1888, young women were being murdered within a mile of each other in the East End of London, and the police had no idea who the killer was or where he would strike next.

Every day the newspapers were full of Ripper news, and details of ongoing police enquiries. Everyone had an opinion on the Ripper's identity — was he a sailor, a local con man, a teacher, even Queen Victoria's grandson Albert, the Duke of Clarence?

 And the truth is...

To this day, no one knows the identity of Jack the Ripper, and no one ever will. Although one Ripper expert pointed the finger at Albert and his friend the Duke of Bedford in the 1960s, there has never been any evidence found to back up his claim. In fact, court documents at the time show Albert had alibis for all but one of the murders, as he was often out of London on the Royal estates at Balmoral and Sandringham.

Verdict: — **BUSTED** —

OTHER (IN)FAMOUS LONDON CRIMINALS

THE KRAY TWINS

Brothers Ronnie and Reggie ran London's criminal underworld from the East End during the 1950s and 1960s until they were arrested and sentenced to life in prison in 1969.

DICK TURPIN

The Essex-born highwayman was basically a robber on horseback, preying on the horse-drawn carriages coming in and out of London. He was arrested and executed in 1739.

THE GREAT TRAIN ROBBERS

Londoner Bruce Reynolds and his gang stole over £2 million in used bank notes from the Glasgow to Euston mail train in 1963. Eventually all the gang were captured and jailed, including Ronnie Biggs who lived in hiding for 30 years!

Foreign visitors to London never actually visit Big Ben

How can this be true? The clock tower that stands at the side of the Palace of Westminster is one of the best known landmarks in London, standing a massive 96 m (316 ft) high and stretching over 16 storeys. The four clock faces are 55 m (180ft) above ground, and are each made from 312 separate pieces of beautifully designed antique glass. You don't need binoculars to see it!

⭐ And the truth is...

Well, Big Ben is actually the nickname given to the Great Bell that's inside the tower. And here's the most interesting bit: despite being one of the world's most famous tourist attractions, the interior of the tower is not open to overseas visitors. UK residents can arrange tours through their local Member of Parliament, but be warned — the tower has 334 stairs. And no lift!

Added to this, no one is quite sure how the Great Bell got its nickname, but most historians agree it was from either Sir Benjamin Hall, who oversaw the bell's installation, the English bare knuckle boxer Benjamin Caunt, a famous sportsman who was the David Beckham of his day.

Verdict: ——— TRUTH

'WOULD YOU ADAM AND EVE IT?'

COCKNEY RHYMING SLANG EXPLAINED

'I haven't seen her in donkey's!'

Donkey's = donkey's ears

Rhymes with years

So 'I haven't seen her in years!'

'He does nothing but rabbit!'

Rabbit = rabbit and pork

Rhymes with talk

So 'He does nothing but talk!'

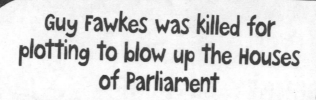

Guy Fawkes was killed for plotting to blow up the Houses of Parliament

We all know the story of Guy Fawkes — the fellow behind the failed Gunpowder Plot to blow up Parliament in 1605. Fawkes and his co-conspirators hatched a plan to kill King James I, and dug a tunnel from a rented house in Whitehall right under the House of Lords that they planned to stuff with enough barrels of gunpowder to make a fireworks night to remember.

Unfortunately for Fawkes and his gang, word of the plan leaked out, and the King sent soldiers to search the tunnels under Parliament. Fawkes was caught, and the gunpowder was discovered. Plotting to kill the King — then as today — is not taken lightly, and all the conspirators were sentenced to rather gruesome deaths.

★ And the truth is...

On 31 January 1606, Fawkes was led to the gallows. Weak from torture, he was helped by the hangman to climb the ladder up the noose. Then, to everyone's surprise, Fawkes jumped off the gallows and broke his neck, thus avoiding the rather horrible punishment that had been planned for him.

Verdict: **BUSTED**

No.5: Roller skates

Young Belgian inventor John Joseph Merlin moved to London in 1760 and opened 'Merlin's Mechanical Museum' to show off his eye-popping inventions — from a wheelchair to a perpetual motion clock to a weighing machine.

Most interesting though were the first known pair of roller skates he built and wore to glide up and down the street outside the museum to attract passers-by. Merlin couldn't quite master his own invention, though, and never learned how to stop. After one accident too many, he discarded the idea and it was eventually patented by a Frenchman, Monsieur Petitbled in 1819.

The bowler hat was invented for businessmen to wear

Let's be honest, the bowler hat is a rather odd piece of headgear. With its distinctive round dome and tiny brim, it looks like you balance it on your head rather than wear it! Nevertheless, the bowler became a part of every City worker's uniform in the 1950s and 1960s, together with a pinstripe suit and a neat leather briefcase. What's more, it's been worn by everyone from Sir Winston Churchill to Princes William and Harry.

★ And the truth is...

The very first bowler was created for Edward Coke, the younger brother of the 2nd Earl of Leicester in 1849 by hat makers Thomas and William Bowler — hence the name. Although the hat may have been adopted by City workers, it was actually first made as safety headgear for workers on country estates, to protect their heads from low-hanging branches when they were out riding. In fact, the story goes that before Coke paid his 12 shillings for the new hat, he put it on the shop floor and stamped on it to make sure it was strong enough!

Verdict: — **BUSTED** —

It's always raining in London!

OK, that's an exaggeration, but it would be fair to say that London is one of the world's wettest cities, wouldn't it? If we were packing for San Francisco, Buenos Aires or Cape Town we'd definitely grab some sunglasses and a pair of swimming trunks. But a trip to London wouldn't be complete without an umbrella.

 ## And the truth is...

Well yes, it does rain quite a lot in London. The Meteorological Office confirms that the number of rainy days in London (with more than 0.25 mm of rainfall) is between 11 and 15 every month. And even worse, one of the rainiest months of the year is August! However, the amount of annual rainfall is considerably lower than lots of other cities around the world that you really wouldn't expect, namely New York, Singapore and Miami. So it's not always raining. It just feels like it!

Verdict: —— BUSTED ——

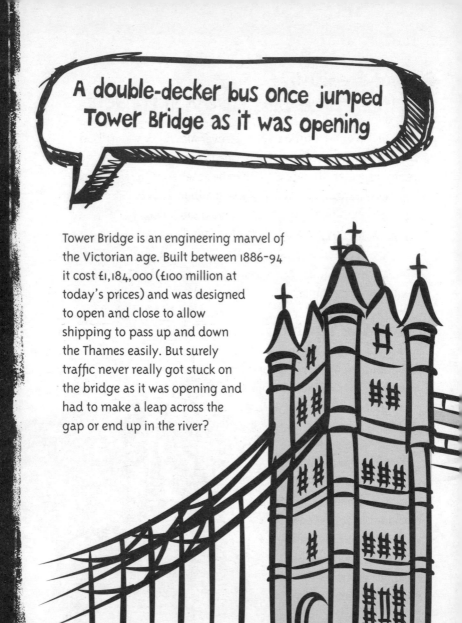

A double-decker bus once jumped Tower Bridge as it was opening

Tower Bridge is an engineering marvel of the Victorian age. Built between 1886-94 it cost £1,184,000 (£100 million at today's prices) and was designed to open and close to allow shipping to pass up and down the Thames easily. But surely traffic never really got stuck on the bridge as it was opening and had to make a leap across the gap or end up in the river?

★ And the truth is...

Actually, that's exactly what did happen! In 1952, a number 78 bus was crossing the bridge when the two walkways started to open. Quick-thinking driver Albert Gunter realised he wouldn't be able to stop in time to prevent the bus falling into the water, so put his foot on the accelerator and jumped the one-metre gap to the other side. Albert and his dozen passengers all escaped the excitement uninjured. And for his next trick, Albert plans to jump the Grand Canyon...

Verdict: ──────── **TRUTH** ────

NO. 10 DOWNING St has 160 rooms!

Call the newspapers! Alert the TV news! The home of the Prime Minister is like Dr Who's Tardis — bigger on the inside than it is on the outside! So does that make the PM a Time Lord?

OK, calm down, and let's examine the facts. Downing Street was built by American Sir George Downing in 1682. With his eye on a quick profit, the property developer erected a few badly built houses, sold them and moved on. In fact, most of the houses have since been destroyed and only Nos 10, 11 and 12 remain of Downing's original terraces.

★ And the truth is...

When they were built, the terraces on Downing Street certainly weren't fit for a Prime Minister. But in 1732, King George II gave No. 10 as a gift to Sir Robert Walpole, the country's first PM, along with a larger and grander house behind No. 10 that faced Horse Guard's Parade. Walpole wasted no time getting the builders to join the two houses together and in 1735, moved into No. 10 Downing Street, which behind its humble front doors actually has a whopping 160 rooms!

Verdict:

© MADE IN... LONDON!

● No.6: Television

If it wasn't for Scottish inventor John Logie Baird we'd have no *Strictly Come Dancing*, no Sky Sports and no *X-Factor*. No, Logie Baird didn't dream up reality shows or the Premier League, he's the brains behind the television set. And more importantly, he invented it above a coffee shop in central London.

That's right, on 27 January 1926 the electronics boffin demonstrated the world's first ever TV broadcast above what is now an Italian coffee shop in Soho. In front of a journalist from *The Times* newspaper and assorted science bigwigs, Logie Baird broadcast live images to his impressed audience.

The Queen never went to school

We can see it now, young Princess Elizabeth setting off from home with a schoolbag over her shoulder, waving goodbye to mum and dad... then nipping round the corner, ditching the books and spending the morning window shopping in the West End, and the afternoon eating popcorn in the local cinema! Are you having a laugh? The Queen playing truant? Of course she went to school!

 ## And the truth is...

Well, actually no, the Queen didn't go to school. But that's not to say she didn't get a first-rate education. Her Majesty was actually educated at home, along with her sister Margaret. And not surprisingly some of the most brilliant academics in the country were queuing up to be her private tutors. The Queen was taught languages by foreign governesses, learned religious studies from none other than the Archbishop of Canterbury, and even had lessons with the Headmaster of Eton.

Verdict: _____

ROYAL BRAIN POWER!

Prince Charles
- degree in anthropology and archaeology from Cambridge University

Prince William
- degree in geography from St Andrews University

Catherine, Duchess of Cambridge
- degree in history of art from St Andrews University

Princess Beatrice
- degree in history and history of ideas from Goldsmiths College, London University

Prince Harry
- 'A' levels in art and geography.

Harrods used to be a fruit and veg shop in east London

Harrods department store in Knightsbridge, West London, is one of the poshest department stores you'll ever come across. Its one million square feet of space and 330 departments attract 15 million visitors per year and contain everything from designer dresses, to rare Italian truffles to gold-plated monkeys (OK, we made that last one up).

★ And the truth is...

Charles Harrod was a tea merchant and grocer who opened his first store in 1834 across the road from his house in Stepney, east London. He moved to Harrods' current site in Knightsbridge in 1849 to be close to the Great Exhibition in Hyde Park. In those early days, Harrods still sold tea and groceries and only employed two staff and a delivery boy. By 1880 though he had expanded, and Harrods was selling everything from medicines and perfume to clothes and exotic food.

Verdict: _____

'WOULD YOU ADAM AND EVE IT?'

COCKNEY RHYMING SLANG EXPLAINED

'Put your weasel on, we're going out'

Weasel = weasel and stoat

Rhymes with coat

So 'Put your coat on, we're going out'

'That's a nice pair of rhythm. Are they new?

Rhythm = rhythm and blues

Rhymes with shoes

So 'That's a nice pair of shoes. Are they new?'

London got its name from the Roman settlement Londinium

There are a few things we know for sure — the Romans arrived in London around AD43 and established the city as a major international trading centre before heading back to Rome in the fifth century. During that time, they built roads, dug early forms of drainage, and created the first river crossings. But did they also give the city its name?

We came, we saw and we called it Londinium!

And the truth is...

No one knows how London got its name, but lots of historians think that the word 'Londinium' is actually pre-Roman and possibly Celtic — from the group of tribes that inhabited the area before the Romans arrived. If that's so, it could have been from King Lud, who named his settlement Kaerlud (meaning Lud's City), or even from the Celtic worlds 'Londo' meaning fierce and 'dun' meaning fort — making it the fierce person's fort!

Verdict: — BUSTED —

© MADE IN... LONDON!

No.7: The tuxedo

In 1860 Savile Row tailors Henry Poole & Co made a short black evening jacket for the Prince of Wales to wear at dinner parties. Six years later an American, James Potter, was invited to attend a party with the Prince and was so impressed with his jacket that before he returned home, he paid Henry Poole to make one for him too!

When Potter returned to New York, he proudly wore his new jacket at the Tuxedo Park Club. Again the jacket proved a huge hit, and fellow members were soon asking their own tailors for a tuxedo.

The Queen's cars don't have number plates

It's fair to say
that the Queen
has a few cars in the
garage at Buckingham Palace.
To start with, there are three vintage
Rolls-Royces — a 1978 Phantom VI that was a gift for her Silver
Jubilee, a 1987 Phantom VI, and the oldest car in the fleet, a 1950
Phantom IV that the Queen still uses to go to Ascot. Surely she's
not driving them all illegally?

 ## And the truth is...

Relax, the Queen is definitely not breaking the law. She has a
fleet of eight State Cars consisting of Bentleys, Rolls-Royces
and Daimler limousines that are used on official engagements
and state visits. These are the only cars in Britain that are not
required by law to display any registration numbers on the
front or rear of the vehicle. The Queen's personal cars, and
those belonging to other members of the Royal Family, all have
number plates.

Verdict:

'WOULD YOU ADAM AND EVE IT?'

COCKNEY RHYMING SLANG EXPLAINED

'Can anyone Lend me some bread?'

Bread = bread and honey

Rhymes with money

So 'Can anyone lend me some money?'

'It's 'taters outside today!'

Taters = potatoes in the mould

Rhymes with cold

So 'It's cold outside today!'

The Queen went on honeymoon with her corgi

The Queen's father, King George VI, introduced Corgis to the Royal Family in 1933 when he bought the first Royal pet, Dookie, from a local kennels. What the Royals saw in these hairy barrels with legs, no one knows, but the Queen was given her own first Corgi, Susan, as an 18th birthday present and still owns three: Monty, Willow and Holly, as well as three Dorgis (a cross between a Corgi and a dachshund): Cider, Candy and Vulcan. We can only imagine what they look like!

 ## And the truth is...

Guilty as charged, my Lord! The Queen married Prince Philip on 20 November 1947 in Westminster Abbey. Coming so soon after the end of the Second World War, the country was still in the middle of austerity measures and the Royal couple honeymooned in Britain. They spent part of the time at Broadlands, Hampshire, the home of Prince Philip's uncle Lord Mountbatten, and part at the Royal estate in Balmoral, Scotland. For the trip to Broadlands, the Queen took Susan along with her. With plenty of dog biscuits for the journey, we hope.

Verdict:  **TRUTH**

© MADE IN... LONDON!

No.8: The sandwich

The perfect marriage of bread, butter and a filling of your choice was invented by John Montagu, the 4th Earl of Sandwich in 1762.

So the story goes, the Earl was a keen gambler, and never wanted to leave the card table while the game was going on in case he missed a good hand. Instead, he would ask his servants to bring him slices of dried meat between two pieces of bread. Gambling friends started to ask for 'the same as Sandwich' and the name stuck.

THE DIRTIEST JOBS IN LONDON!

One thing's for sure, if you wanted to earn a few quid in old London, you couldn't be afraid of getting your hands dirty...

1 Resurrection men

This is another way of saying 'body snatcher', which is a person who dug up dead bodies from graveyards and sold them to medical students to experiment on. The problem was, 19th century laws only released around 50 bodies per year to medical science, but students needed closer to 500! Body snatching became such a thriving business that relatives started standing guard over the graves of their loved ones, and even burying them in locked iron coffins!

2 Mudlarks

As the name suggests, these enterprising treasure hunters — usually teenage boys and girls — would wade through the mud, raw sewage and corpses (yes, corpses!) on the banks of the Thames, scavenging for any valuables that had been washed up. Old bottles, copper nails dropped from ships — everything they could find was collected and sold.

3 Soot bag men

These off-duty chimney sweeps were employed by the
railways before the days of ticket inspectors. A soot bag
man would be sent into third class train carriages to empty
his sooty sheets on the other passengers. Anyone who could
afford to travel in second and first class would quickly
escape to better carriages and pay a higher fare!

4 Violin string maker

It was the violin string maker's job to turn the lower
intestines of a sheep into strings fit for a Stradivarius*. First
of all, he would slice open the sheep's stomach, remove the
fatty tissue, blood vessels and bile, and clean the intestines.
The thinner ends were twisted together and dried to make
violin strings. The thicker bits went off to make sausage
skins. Not a job for vegetarians.

*Generally regarded as the world's best violin

London is full of secret bomb shelters

During WWII, the German air force spent nearly a year bombing London and other cities night after night. More than one million homes were destroyed in London and more than 20,000 Londoners were killed. And that wasn't soldiers; it was women and children, and people too old or sick to be called up to fight.

If there was enough notice of an attack, or air raid as it was known, people would often leave their homes and take shelter in underground stations. But some of these are deeper and therefore safer than others, plus cramming all those people onto platforms wasn't easy. So, the story goes, the government commissioned ten secret deep-level shelters to protect as many Londoners as possible during air raids.

And the truth is...

Eight shelters were completed and opened in 1942 — at Belsize Park, Camden Town, Goodge Street, Chancery Lane, Stockwell, Clapham North, Clapham Common and Clapham South. Two other shelters were started at St Paul's and the Oval, but never finished. Each shelter held up to 8,000 people and during WWII they even hosted US General Eisenhower. The shelters can still be seen today — if you know where to look.

Verdict:  TRUTH

The Thames didn't used to flow through London

Without the Thames there would be no London. History boffins reckon the Thames valley was first inhabited as far back as the Bronze Age 400,000 years ago. And when the Romans invaded Britain they expanded London into an international port, and built the first crossing point over the river — the original London Bridge. So how could this all have happened if the Thames wasn't flowing through London?

 ## And the truth is...

Rewind 30 million years and the river we know today as the Thames, was actually a tributary* of the German River Rhine. This is because at that time, Britain wasn't even an island — it was still attached to mainland Europe.

The original Thames flowed from the Midlands, through Oxfordshire, Hertfordshire and joined the European mainland at Ipswich on the Suffolk coast. Then during the Ice Age 10,000 years ago (practically five minutes when you consider the history of the Earth) a massive glacier blocked its path, causing the river to alter its course and start to follow the route we know today.

Basically a small branch or offshoot

Verdict:

London's first shopping mall was on the Thames

You can't move for shopping centres these days. And developers seem to build them anywhere. But here at **TRUTH OR BUSTED**, we can't see how even the most inventive shopkeepers could manage to open a shop on the River Thames — without everything sinking or floating away!

 ## And the truth is...

In pre-nineteenth-century London, extremely cold winters would sometimes cause the Thames to freeze over. During the Great Frost of 1683-84, the lowest temperatures ever recorded in England, the Thames was completely frozen for two months, with ice reaching a thickness of 28 cm (11 in).

'Frost Fairs' were held on the ice, with stalls open for locals to buy food and drink, and even mini-theatres to watch plays! The last fair was in 1814 and it's unlikely there will ever be another one, because the river now flows too fast for the water to freeze.

Verdict:

Shops that could have existed at the Frost Fair

(Tide)
Marks and
Spencer

ICELAND

OASIS

(Snow)
Boots The
Chemist

River Island
(geddit?)

Smog once killed 12,000 people in London

Smog — a cross between smoke and fog — is a type of air pollution, caused by a mixture of car exhaust fumes and the smoke from factories and home coal fires. The winter of 1952 was unusually cold in London, and the smoke from around one million coal-fired stoves caused a heavy fog and poor air quality over the city. Sulphur dioxide levels were seven times higher than normal, and for five days visibility was below 500 m.

★ And the truth is...

The smog reacted with the sulphur dioxide to form sulphuric acid!* Londoners starting dying of pneumonia, bronchitis and heart failure, with deaths peaking at 900 per day on 8 and 9 December. Within two weeks, 4,000 people were dead, and over the course of the winter the total rose to 12,000. The only good news was that it prompted the government to pass the Clean Air Act, offering families money to switch from coal to electric fires, and cracking down on the emissions from factories.

Verdict:

TRUTH

* A strong acid used in car batteries

No.9: Traffic lights

BEWARE OF EXPLOSIONS

Railway engineer John Peake Knight invented the first traffic light in London in 1868. Knight's invention wasn't the red/amber/green box we know today, but a revolving gas-powered contraption with just a red and green light similar to railway signals at the time.

Nevertheless, Knight's brainchild was quickly adopted and the first traffic light was installed near the House of Commons, on the corner of George Street and Bridge Street. Unfortunately, the light exploded in 1869, injuring a policeman who was operating it, and the traffic light was removed the following year!

Fortnum & Mason is the Queen's local grocer

Fortnum & Mason is one of London's most historic and upmarket shops. Selling teas, coffees, Christmas hampers, and all kinds of exotic groceries from scotch eggs to caviar, it's like a food department store, and it's existed on the same site in Piccadilly since 1707. But has the Queen ever popped down there for a loaf and a pint of milk?

 ## And the truth is...

You're unlikely to find the Queen pushing a trolley around the aisles, but the store is a holder of a Royal Warrant, which means it supplies goods to the Royal household. Queen Victoria actually sent shipments of Fortnum & Mason's concentrated beef tea to Florence Nightingale's hospitals during the Crimean War to cheer up the patients! Today the Royal Family are said to be fond of Fortnum & Mason's famous hampers for annual events such as the Henley Regatta and Ascot Races.

The store's Royal connections began with William Fortnum, who was a footman for Queen Anne, before retiring from Royal service to go into business with a friend Hugh Mason.

Verdict:

WALLET STRETCHERS

Five of Fortnum & Mason's most exotic groceries

FOIE GRAS EN CROUTE
(Duck Liver Pate Pie)
£320

FARMED BELUGA CAVIAR
£250

FORTNUM'S FAVOURITES CHOCOLATES
£65

WILD BALTIC ROYAL SALMON FILLET
£60

IMPERIAL CHRISTMAS HAMPER
£5,000

WEIRD LANDMARKS

Here are a few spots you won't find in the guide books...

False teeth museum

The Hunterian Museum is the personal collection of 18th century surgeon John Hunter and includes a 7ft 7in man's skeleton, the tooth of an extinct giant sloth, and Winston Churchill's false teeth.

Non-existent Peter Pan statue

The statue in Kensington Gardens of the 'boy who never grew up' was built and erected by the *Peter Pan* author J M Barrie in 1912 without council permission, meaning it doesn't officially exist. Visit it one day and let us know if you can officially see it.

Wedding cake steeple

The distinctive steeple of St Bride's Church in Fleet Street inspired a baker working in a shop opposite to invent the multi-tiered wedding cake design used today.

Head drilling apparatus

The Old Operating Theatre Museum is just that — an old operating theatre containing many gruesome reminders of the days before anaesthetic. Include devices for trepanning — drilling a hole in the skull, as a cure for headaches. Ouch.

Very small grave

Penniless practical joker playwright Ben Jonson was buried 'standing up' in Westminster Abbey because it was cheaper to pay for a 2 ft x 2 ft hole!

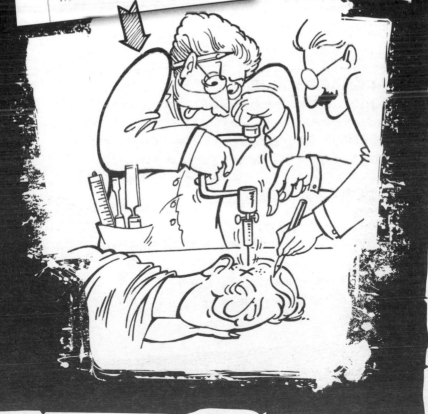

The Royal Family lives in Buckingham Palace

If we had to bet on any of the statements in this book, it'd be this one. It's a dead cert, isn't it? Buckingham Palace has been the main Royal residence since Queen Victoria moved in back in 1837. The house has actually been in Royal hands even longer, since Sir Charles Sheffield sold it to George III for £21,000 (more like £3 million in today's money) in 1761.

★ And the truth is...

Despite having a rather impressive 775 rooms, Buckingham Palace is often not occupied by the Royal Family. The house is actually only the official London residence of the Queen, Prince Philip and two of their children, Prince Andrew and Prince Edward, while other Royals are dotted around various other London locations.

Plus the Queen and Prince Philip do tend to travel about a bit, spending Christmas until February at Sandringham House in Norfolk, August and September at Balmoral Castle in Scotland. They also deposit their suitcases at Windsor Castle in Berkshire for a month over Easter and a week in June for Royal Ascot!

Verdict: **BUSTED**

ORF-FICIAL RESIDENCES

CLARENCE HOUSE
Built between 1825-27 for Prince William Henry, the Duke of Clarence. Today it's home to The Prince of Wales, the Duchess of Cornwall and Prince Harry. When he's home.

ST JAMES'S PALACE
Built by King Henry VIII between 1531-36, this is the London home of the Princess Royal (Anne) and Princess Beatrice of York.

KENSINGTON PALACE
Birthplace of Queen Victoria, this was the official home to generations of kings and queens before the move to Buckingham Palace. It now counts the Duke and Duchess of Cambridge as its official residents.

> # There are over 40 'ghosts' on the London Underground

Anyone who has spent Monday morning on the Underground would certainly admit to seeing a few pasty-looking commuters on the way in to work. But ghosts? We've never heard any wailing or chains rattling.

⭐ And the truth is...

By ghosts, we mean abandoned or 'ghost' stations. And believe us, there are loads of them! Aldwych station, which opened in 1907 to shuttle trains backwards and forwards to Holborn, closed in 1994, and Down Street station, near Hyde Park Corner, was also opened in 1907 and closed again in 1932.

One of the most interesting 'ghosts' is Bull & Bush, which was designed to be the deepest station on the whole tube network, but was abandoned before it was even completed. Look out the tube window between Hampstead and Golders Green and you might even catch a glimpse of the half-built platform. Spooky!

Verdict:  TRUTH

London taxis <u>have</u> to stop when their yellow light is on

If you live in London, or you've ever visited, you'll be familiar with the sight of black cabs buzzing around the street. They are the only form of transport licensed by the Public Carriage Office to be able to stop in the street to pick up passengers. Just stand on the pavement, stick out your arm and wait for one with their yellow light on (meaning they're empty) to stop and pick you up.

★ And the truth is...

Some of you might have experienced this — the surprise/annoyance/frustration of seeing a cab with its yellow light on drive past and leave you on the pavement. Well actually, cab drivers are perfectly within their rights to do this, and are NOT obliged to stop when flagged down. One thing you should know, though, is that once a driver has stopped, he must accept your fare unless you're travelling over 6 miles (10 km). Or going south of the river, as the joke goes.

Verdict:  BUSTED

81

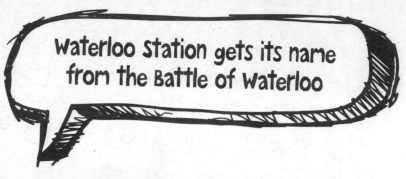

Waterloo Station gets its name from the Battle of Waterloo

Waterloo Station opened in 1922 and is the second busiest station in Europe behind Paris Gare du Nord. It carries 88 million passengers per year to Surrey, Berkshire, Hampshire and the South-West. But was it named after Napoleon's famous defeat in 1815 at the hands of allied forces led by the Duke of Wellington?

★ And the truth is...

Erm, no. Waterloo Station started life as Waterloo Bridge Station, taking its name from the nearby river crossing. However, Waterloo Bridge was named after the famous British victory, so not far off.

Verdict: Nearly true, but actually  BUSTED

'WOULD YOU ADAM AND EVE IT?'

COCKNEY RHYMING SLANG EXPLAINED

'Jane fell down the apples and broke her chalk'

Apples = apples and pears

Rhymes with stairs

Chalk = Chalk Farm*

Rhymes with arm

So 'Jane fell down the stairs and broke her arm'

* An area of London near Camden Town

'I wanted to go out, but I haven't got a sausage'

Sausage = sausage and mash

Rhymes with cash

So 'I wanted to go out, but I haven't got any cash'

BRICKS AND MORTAR

WELCOME TO THE SMALLEST, WEIRDEST AND PRICIEST HOUSES IN LONDON!

STRANGEST SHAPE

South Kensington is one of London's poshest areas. But you'd have to really want to live there, to squeeze yourself into this wedge-shaped terrace on Thurloe Square. The cheese-shaped chunk of real estate starts tiny and gets wider, like the Flatiron Building in New York.

MOST EXPENSIVE

Britain's richest man Lakshmi Mittal set a UK record when he paid £117m for a property next door to the Sultan of Brunei and Kensington Palace — an area better known as Billionaire's Boulevard. The impressive pad, which Mittal bought for his son Aditya (yes please, Dad!) has four floors, its own art gallery, and a garage that is not only large enough for 20 cars, but is also lined with the same marble that was used to build the Taj Mahal.

MOST SQUASHED

Lay off the stodgy pies if you're planning a trip here, because this five-storey building on the Goldhawk Road in West London measures just 1.5m (5 ft 5in) wide at its narrowest point! The former hat shop was built by crackpot Victorian architects who wanted to experiment with space saving, and so constructed a house in the gap between two existing buildings.

SKINNIEST

You've heard the expression 'Not enough room to swing a cat'? Well, 10 Hyde Park Place, near Marble Arch, could have inspired that. Why? Because at 1 m (3 ft, 6in) wide, you could barely squeeze through the door wearing shoulder pads, let alone raise your pet moggy aloft! Built in 1805, the house was never designed to be lived in, but acted as a guard house to prevent graverobbers stealing corpses from nearby St George's cemetery!

The Thames is too polluted for fish to live in it

For centuries, the river that flowed through Britain's capital city was as dirty and smelly as a Glastonbury festival toilet. In 1878, 600 passengers on the steamship *Princess Alice* died when their boat sank and — although they all escaped — they couldn't swim to shore because the pollution was too bad! As recently as 1957, water quality was so bad that the river was declared biologically dead, and even the river banks stank of rotten eggs.

★ And the truth is...

The government was shamed into passing strict laws on pollution, and now the Thames is the cleanest it has been for 150 years. Environmentalists reckon there are more than 100 different species of fish thriving in the river, as well as sea birds, seals and even dolphins. In the last 30 years new breeds of fish have been introduced, including chub, roach and bream. In 2003 a fly fisherman even caught a large trout next to a council tip in Wandsworth!

Verdict: —— BUSTED ——

It's impossible to swim straight across the Thames

In 2011, newspaper columnist Matthew Parris tried to swim across the Thames from his flat to see if he could reach Limehouse opposite. Misreading the tides he ended up three-quarters of a mile upstream and had to walk back home dripping wet and barefoot. Did Parris just make a boob, or are Thames' tides just too strong for swimmers to cope with?

 And the truth is...

People might think that taking to the tidal Thames is a bit like playing with the traffic on a motorway, but as recently as the 1940s there was actually a public beach at London Bridge, where families went to swim and bathe. And it's still perfectly legal to swim in the Thames. The problems come from the river traffic (no one wants to get bumped by a barge), and the strong tidal currents.

Verdict:

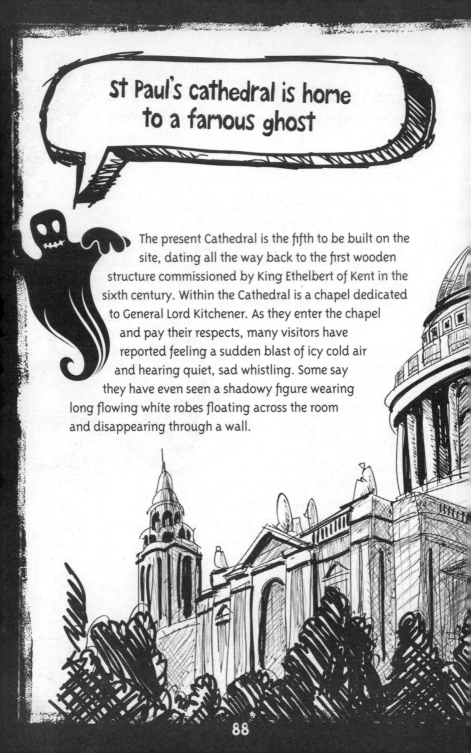

St Paul's cathedral is home to a famous ghost

The present Cathedral is the fifth to be built on the site, dating all the way back to the first wooden structure commissioned by King Ethelbert of Kent in the sixth century. Within the Cathedral is a chapel dedicated to General Lord Kitchener. As they enter the chapel and pay their respects, many visitors have reported feeling a sudden blast of icy cold air and hearing quiet, sad whistling. Some say they have even seen a shadowy figure wearing long flowing white robes floating across the room and disappearing through a wall.

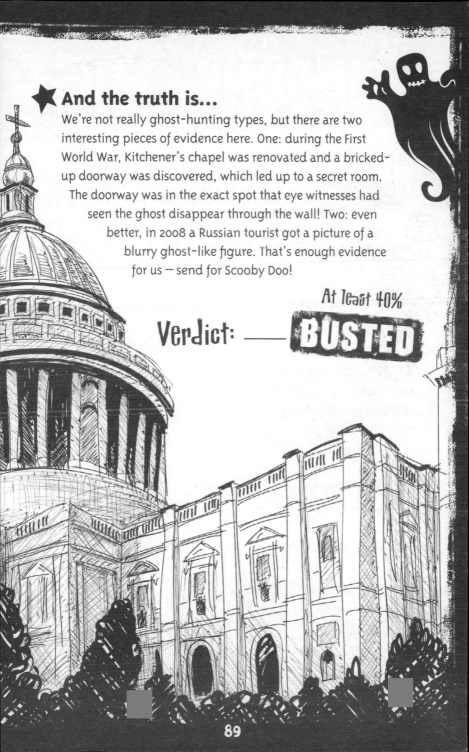

★ And the truth is...

We're not really ghost-hunting types, but there are two interesting pieces of evidence here. One: during the First World War, Kitchener's chapel was renovated and a bricked-up doorway was discovered, which led up to a secret room. The doorway was in the exact spot that eye witnesses had seen the ghost disappear through the wall! Two: even better, in 2008 a Russian tourist got a picture of a blurry ghost-like figure. That's enough evidence for us – send for Scooby Doo!

At least 40%

Verdict: —— **BUSTED**

LONDON'S MOST

1 THE QUEEN'S HOUSE, GREENWICH

In 1966 a pair of Canadian tourists, the Reverend and Mrs Hardy, photographed two ghosts on the stairs of this historic house that was originally built for the wife of King Charles I.

2 SUTTON HOUSE, HACKNEY

Neighbours report that dogs are often heard wailing and barking from inside this historic Tudor House in the dead of night. But no dogs live there! Apparently live dogs are scared rigid by the place, too, and refuse to enter the house.

3 HANDEL'S HOUSE MUSEUM, MAYFAIR

Composer Handel lived here from 1723 until his death in 1759. When the house was being restored in 2000, builders were confronted by not one but two ghostly presences — thought to be singers who worked regularly with the composer.

HAUNTED HOUSES!

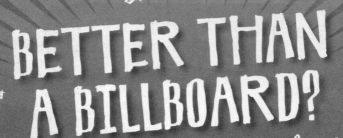

BETTER THAN A BILLBOARD?

These London landmarks are famous for advertising food to flights

The BT Tower

This space-age looking 189 m (620 ft) tower was London's tallest building until 1980. The BT Tower, originally built for the Post Office in 1966, but now owned and renamed by British Telecom, has a revolving restaurant at the top, and contains the TV Network Switching Centre (which juggles TV signals from channels, advertisers and international satellite services to make sure that shows and adverts happen in the right order).

The OXO Tower

Originally built as a power station for the Post Office in the late nineteenth century, the building was bought by the Leibig Extract of Meat Company, who made OXO cubes. They wanted a tower with illuminated signs advertising their product, but when permission was refused they installed three vertical windows on each face of the tower, in the shape of a circle, a cross and a circle, making the OXO Tower London's biggest billboard!

The Emirates Stadium

Arsenal Football Club used to play at an old-fashioned ground called Highbury. But club bigwigs decided they could make more money if they moved to a purpose-built stadium five minutes down the road. And then they realised they could make even more money if they sold the naming rights to the stadium for £100m! Emirates airlines signed a 15-year deal to put their name on the stadium and the team's shirts.

The Hoover Building

As its name suggests, the Hoover Building in West London was once a factory making vacuum cleaners for the Hoover company. During WWII, the government asked Hoover to switch production to electrical parts for aircraft and tanks. By the early 1980s, Hoover had moved their factories outside London, and eventually Tesco bought the site and built a supermarket behind it. However, because the building's design is historically important, the whopping great sign 'Hoover Building' stayed on the front and keeps advertising the company's vacuum cleaners!

Where can I find myths about...

100%
SUCKER-PROOF

GUARANTEED!

Take a look at our other marvellously mythbusting titles...

Tip:
Turn over!